THE COOK'S COLLECTION
❋

SUCCESSFUL
BAKING

Author: Annette Wolter
Photography: Rolf Feuz and Karin Messerli
Translated by UPS Translations, London
Edited by Josephine Bacon

CLB 4162
This edition published in 1995 by Grange Books
an imprint of Grange Books PLC, The Grange, Grange Yard, London SE1 3AG
This material published originally under the series title "Kochen Wie Noch Nie"
by Gräfe und Unzer Verlag GmbH, München
© 1995 Gräfe und Unzer Verlag GmbH, München
English translation copyright: © 1995 by CLB Publishing, Godalming, Surrey
Typeset by Image Setting, Brighton, E. Sussex
Printed and bound in Singapore
ISBN 1-85627-760-7

THE COOK'S COLLECTION
❈

SUCCESSFUL
BAKING

Annette Wolter

Grange
BOOKS

Introduction

Bread-making is a wonderfully therapeutic craft, and one that should be encouraged in these days of stressful rushing from one appointment to another. Bread is a great stimulant of the senses. It is lovely to feel the elastic dough in one's hands, there is nothing to compare with the welcoming smell of home-baked bread filling the house, and nothing quite as tempting as a slice of bread, warm from the oven, spread with a generous layer of fresh butter. Freshly baked bread, although wonderful eaten on the day it is made, also freezes well and so is suitable for making in large quantities.

The basic process for making leavened bread involves mixing wheat flour with warm water and yeast and then kneading the dough to develop the gluten in the flour. Kneading is the rhythmic pulling and pushing of the dough until it feels sufficiently springy and elastic. The better the dough is kneaded, the lighter the finished product will turn out. After kneading, the dough is covered and put aside to rise in a warm place. The risen dough is then punched back and kneaded a little more before being shaped ready for the oven, left again to rise, and then baked.

While traditional bread baking can be a joy, there is no shame in turning to modern kitchen implements when time is limited. Electric mixers and food processors make light work of blending and kneading the ingredients. Whichever method you adopt, the finished product will be irresistible.

This selection of breads, rolls and delicious savouries offers the cook a delightful choice of recipes. There are croissants and brioches that turn the everyday breakfast into a special treat fit for guests; robust wholemeal loaves, speciality breads from foreign lands, and savoury bites to accompany drinks.

For those who love baking, this collection will provide new ideas. For those who have yet to experience the simple pleasure of producing their first loaf, this book will surely inspire many to take up this age-old craft.

Sesame Bread

Quantities for 2 loaves:
500g/1lb 2oz rye flakes
2 tbsps sourdough mix
750ml/11/4 pints lukewarm
water
250g/8oz wheatmeal flour
500g/1lb 2oz rye flour
2 packets dry yeast
4 tbsps sesame seeds
1 tbsp salt
Baking paper for the baking
sheet

Preparation time:
45 minutes
Rising time:
13 hours
Baking time:
40 minutes
Nutritional value:
Analysis per slice, if divided
into 50 slices, approx
• 335kJ/80kcal
• 2g protein
• 1g fat
• 16g carbohydrate

Combine the rye flakes, the sourdough mix and 500ml/18 fl oz water. Cover and leave for 12 hours at room temperature. Add the rest of the lukewarm water, both types of flour, the dry yeast, 3 tbsps sesame seeds and the salt to the starter dough. Knead to a workable dough. If the dough is too wet, add more wheatmeal flour. • Cover and leave to rise in a warm place for 1 hour. • Line the baking sheet with greaseproof paper. • Flour your hands and shape the dough into 2 long loaves, place them on the baking sheet, brush with cold water and sprinkle with the remaining sesame seeds. • Bake the bread on the bottom shelf of a preheated 200°C/400°F/Gas Mark 6 oven for 40 minutes. Cool on a wire rack.

Hazelnut Wholemeal Bread

Quantities for 1 large loaf:
150g/5¹/₂oz hazelnuts
750g/1lb 11oz wholewheat flour
250g/8oz whole rye flour
42g/1¹/₂oz fresh yeast or 21g/3/4 oz dry yeast
500ml/18 fl oz lukewarm sour milk or kefir
Pinch of sugar
150g/5¹/₂oz sourdough (see tip)
1 tbsp sea salt
2 tsps freshly ground coriander seed
100ml/4 fl oz lukewarm water
1 tbsp pinhead oatmeal
Butter for the baking sheet

Preparation time:
30 minutes
Rising time:
2 hours
Baking time:
1 hour and 5 minutes
Nutritional value:
Analysis per slice, if divided into 30 slices, approx:
•670kJ/160kcal
• 6g protein
• 5g fat
• 25g carbohydrate

Coarsely chop the hazelnuts. • Combine the flours in a large bowl and make a well in the centre. Crumble the yeast into the well, add a little sour milk and the sugar and mix together, incorporating only a little flour. If using dry yeast, blend the yeast with the sugar and 125ml/4 fl oz sour milk and then pour onto the flour. Sprinkle the yeast mixture with a little flour. Cover and leave in a warm place until little cracks can be seen in the flour on the surface. This should take about 15 minutes. • Knead into the dough the remaining sour milk, hazelnuts, sourdough, salt, coriander and as much water as is required to form a moist dough. More water or flour can be added if necessary. • Cover the dough and leave it to rise in a warm place for about 1 hour and 15 minutes, during which time it should double in bulk. • Butter a baking sheet. • Knead the dough thoroughly once again, shape into a loaf and place it on the baking sheet. Cover and leave to prove for a further

30 minutes. • Brush the loaf with cold water and sprinkle with the pinhead oatmeal, pressing it down gently.with the back of a wooden spoon • Preheat the oven to 200°C/400°F/Gas Mark 6. Place an ovenproof dish containing cold water in the base of the oven. Bake the bread on the bottom shelf for 45 minutes. Reduce the temperature to 180°C/350°F/Gas Mark 4 and bake the bread for a further 20 minutes. To check if the bread is done, remove it from the oven and, holding it upside down in a cloth, tap the underside. If it sounds hollow it is properly baked. Leave to cool on a wire rack.

Our Tip: *Bread which is baked using sourdough remains fresh for longer than bread baked only with yeast. You can make the sourdough from a starter which can be purchased in some health food stores or baker's shops. Alternatively you can make the sourdough yourself from scratch. To do this, mix 75g/3oz rye flour with 1 tsp sugar or honey and 125ml/4 fl oz lukewarm water. Cover the mixture with a cloth and leave in a warm place for 3 to 5 days until bubbles form and the mixture smells sour. Stir the mixture every now and then. The sourdough can be kept in a tightly sealed container in the refrigerator for up to 2 weeks.*

Hand-shaped Wheaten Bread

Quantities for 2 loaves:
1.5kg/3lbs organic wholemeal
flour
1 tsp salt
84g/3oz fresh yeast or
42g/1¹/₂oz dry yeast
250g/8oz wheatmeal flour
1 tsp sugar
2 tbsps wheatgerm
500ml/18 fl oz lukewarm
water
4 tbsps milk
Baking paper for the baking
sheet

Preparation time:
30 minutes
Rising time:
1 hour 45 minutes
Baking time:
50 minutes
Nutritional value:
Analysis per slice, if 2 loaves
divided into 50 slices, approx:
• 460kJ/110kcal
• 4g protein
• 1g fat
• 22g carbohydrate

Combine the wholemeal flour and salt in a bowl, cover and leave in a warm place. • Crumble the fresh yeast over the flour, mix with the sugar, a little water and the flour. If using dry yeast, blend with the sugar and water and pour this over the flour. Cover and leave to rise in a warm place for 30 minutes. • Knead the wheatmeal flour, wheatgerm and the remaining water into the yeast mixture. Knead the dough until smooth and elastic and then leave to rise in a warm place for 45 minutes. • Line the baking sheet with baking paper. • Knead the dough with floured hands. Shape it into two loaves. Place them on the baking sheet, cover and leave to prove for 30 minutes. • Place a dish of cold water on the oven floor. • Make four cuts across the tops of the loaves and brush with milk. Bake on the bottom shelf of a preheated 220°C/425°F/Gas Mark 7 oven for 50 minutes or until golden brown.

Wheatmeal Loaf

Quantities for 1 30cm/12in loaf:
750g/1lb 11oz wholewheat flour
750g/1lb 11oz wheatmeal flour
2 tbsps wheatgerm
63g/2¹/₂oz fresh yeast or 32g/1oz dry yeast
500ml/18 fl oz lukewarm water
1 tsp salt
1 tbsp melted butter
Oil for the tin

Preparation time:
30 minutes
Rising time:
14 hours
Baking time:
50 minutes
Nutritional value:
Analysis per slice, if divided into 30 slices, approx:
• 670kJ/160kcal
• 6g protein
• 1g fat
• 31g carbohydrate

Combine the flours in a bowl, add the wheatgerm and make a well in the centre. Crumble the fresh yeast into the well. Add 400ml/14 fl oz water and a little flour and mix to a dough. If using dry yeast, blend the yeast with the 400ml/14 fl oz water, add a little flour and pour into the well. Sprinkle a little flour on top and leave to rise in a warm place for 12 hours. • Mix the milk with the rest of the water and the salt and combine with this starter and the rest of the flours to form a workable dough. Cover and leave to rise for 1 hour. • Knead the dough thoroughly again, place in the oiled tin and leave to rise for a further hour. • Make a 5mm/¹/₄in deep cut lengthways in the dough and brush the top with the melted butter. Preheat the oven to 230°C/450°F/Gas Mark 8. Place a cupful of water in the base of the oven. Bake the bread on the bottom shelf for 50 minutes.

Herbed Oaten Bread
with Sunflower Seeds

Quantities for 1 loaf:
500g/1lb 2oz wholewheat
flour
100g/4oz rolled oats
63g/2¹/₂oz fresh yeast or
32g/1oz dry yeast
250ml/9 fl oz lukewarm water
Pinch of sugar
125g/5oz sunflower seeds
175g/6oz thick-set plain
yogurt
1 tsp sea salt
¹/₂ tsp ground coriander
1 tsp each dried thyme and
rosemary
Butter for the baking sheet

Preparation time:
30 minutes
Rising time:
1 hour
Baking time:
1 hour
Nutritional value:
Analysis per slice, if divided
into 25 slices, approx:
• 460kJ/110kcal
• 5g protein
• 3g fat
•16g carbohydrate

Combine the flour and
rolled oats. Crumble the
fresh yeast into the middle,
mix with 4 tbsps water and the
sugar and sprinkle with a little
flour. Cover and leave to rise
for 15 minutes. If using dry
yeast, make a well in the
centre of the flour, blend the
yeast with the water and sugar
and then pour the mixture into
the well. • Reserve 1 tbsp of
the sunflower seeds and
coarsely chop the rest. Add
these, together with the
remaining water, yogurt, salt,
coriander, crushed thyme and
rosemary, to the starter dough
and the rest of the flour.
Knead well. The dough should
be moist, but should leave the
sides of the bowl clean. Cover
and leave the dough to rise in
a warm place until it has
doubled in bulk. • Butter the
baking sheet. • Knead the
dough again, shape it into a

12

loaf, place on the baking sheet, cover and leave to prove for 15 minutes. • Make ½cm/¼in cuts in the top of the dough in a grid pattern, brush the dough with water and sprinkle with the remaining sunflower seeds. • Bake on the centre shelf of a preheated 200°C/400°F/Gas Mark 6 oven for 1 hour. Test to see if it is done and leave to cool on a wire rack.

Wholemeal Bread
in a Clay Pot

Quantities for 1 large clay pot:
For the sourdough:
250g/8oz wholewheat flour
2 tsps dry yeast
250ml/9 fl oz lukewarm water
2 tbsps clear honey
For the starter dough:
250g/8oz wholewheat
250ml/9 fl oz lukewarm water
For the bread dough:
125g/5oz cracked wheat
750ml/1¼ pints water
*700g/1lb 10oz wholewheat
flour*
1 tsp seasoned salt
1 tbsp fines herbs
Oil for greasing the clay pot

Preparation time:
1 hour
Rising time:
36 hours
Baking time:
1¾ hours
Nutritional value:
Analysis per slice, if divided
into 40 slices, approx:
•420kJ/100kcal
• 42g protein
•10g fat
• 21g carbohydrate

To make the sourdough, mix the wholewheat flour with the dry yeast, lukewarm water and honey. Cover and leave in a warm place, at about 24°C/75°F, for 24 hours. The surface of the mixture should then resemble pale, fluffy foam. If it has a pink or red growth, discard it and start again • Add the flour and water for the starter dough and mix with the sourdough. Cover and leave for a further 12 hours. The dough should be slightly foaming and have the characteristic yeasty smell. • Immerse the clay pot and lid in cold water for 1½ hours. • Boil the 125g/5oz cracked wheat in the water on a low heat in a covered pan for 30 minutes, switch off the heat and leave to stand for a further 30 minutes. Drain the grains and add to the starter dough. • Add the rest of the wholewheat flour to the starter dough, together with the salt and fines herbes. Knead well. The dough will be a little sticky. • Drain the clay pot and brush well with oil. • Transfer

the dough to the clay pot, smooth the top, cover with a cloth and leave to rise in a warm place for at least 2 hours. Once risen, the dough should have increased in bulk by about one-third. • Cover the pot with its lid. Place a shelf on the oven floor, put the clay pot in the cold oven and turn the oven to 200°C/400°F/Gas Mark 6. • Bake the bread for 50 minutes, then remove the lid and continue baking for a further 40 minutes or until lightly browned. The bread should have shrunk away from the pot a little on all sides. • Switch off the oven and leave the bread in it for 15 minutes. Remove it from the pot, spray it all over with cold water and cool on a wire rack.

Our Tip: Bread baked in a clay pot has a very aromatic flavour and is generally of fine texture. Wholewheat bread is best left to stand for a day before slicing. If stored in a cool, well-ventilated place it will keep fresh for a week.

Rye Potato Bread

Quantities for 1 30cm/12in baking tin:
For the starter dough:
200g/7oz rye flour
2 tsps dry yeast
400ml/14 fl oz lukewarm water
2 tsps clear honey
For the bread dough:
500g/1lb 2oz floury potatoes
350g/11oz wholewheat flour
50g/2oz soya flour
200ml/7 fl oz lukewarm water
1 tsp each caraway seeds, sea salt and dried marjoram
Butter for the tin

Preparation time:
40 minutes
Rising time:
26 hours
Baking time:
1 hour 5 minutes
Nutritional value:
Analysis per slice, if divided into 30 slices, approx:
• 290kJ/70kcal
• 3g protein
• 1g fat
• 14g carbohydrate

To make the starter dough, mix the rye flour with the dry yeast, water and honey. • Cover with a cloth and leave for at least 24 hours in a warm place at 24°C/75°F. By this time the dough should clearly be fermenting and will resemble a pale, fluffy foam. • Prior to baking the bread, scrub the potatoes under running water and boil them in their skins for 30-35 minutes or until soft. • Peel the cooked potatoes immediately and grate them. • Mix the grated potato into the starter dough. • Add the wholewheat flour to the starter dough, together with the caraway seeds, salt and crushed marjoram. Knead to a workable dough. • Butter the tin, place the dough in it and smooth the top with a spatula. Leave the dough to rise in a warm place until it has increased in bulk by one-third. This will take 1 to 2 hours. • Place the tin on the bottom shelf of a preheated

200°C/400°F/Gas Mark 6 oven and bake for 50 minutes or until golden brown. Then turn off the oven and leave the bread to rest in the oven for a further 15 minutes. • Remove the rye potato bread from the tin, spray the top with cold water and leave to cool on a wire rack.

Our Tip: *Leave the bread for 24 hours before slicing. When a little stale it is delicious toasted. If you enjoy experimenting, try making this bread with grated courgette, beetroot or carrot. Use the same quantity as for potato, i.e. 500g/1lb 2oz. It may be necessary to adjust the amount of added liquid.*

French Bread

Quantities for 5 French loaves:
1kg/2½lbs strong plain flour
42g/1½oz fresh yeast or
21g/¾oz dry yeast
Pinch of sugar
750ml/1¼ pints lukewarm
water
3 tsps salt
½ tsp ground aniseed (optional)
Flour for the baking sheet

Preparation time:
30 minutes
Rising time:
1½ hours
Baking time:
45 minutes
Nutritional value:
Analysis per loaf, approx:
• 2890kJ/690kcal
• 22g protein
• 2g fat
• 150g carbohydrate

Sift the flour into a warmed bowl, make a well in the centre and crumble the fresh yeast into it. Sprinkle the sugar on top and mix in the water and a little flour. If using dry yeast, blend the yeast with the sugar and water and a little flour before pouring into the well. • Sprinkle a little flour over the starter dough, cover and leave to rise in a warm place at about 22°C/70°F for 15 minutes or until cracks appear in the flour. Add the salt and aniseed, if using, and knead all the ingredients until the dough is smooth and elastic. Cover and leave to rise in a warm place for 1 hour or until doubled in bulk. • Dust the baking sheets with flour. • Knead the dough again on a lightly floured surface and divide into 5 equal portions. • Roll each into a 50cm/20in French stick, place on the baking sheet, cover and leave to rise for a further 15 minutes. • Brush the loaves with lukewarm water, make 5 ½cm/¼in deep diagonal cuts in each loaf and bake on the centre shelf of a preheated 220°C/425°F/Gas Mark 7 oven for 45 minutes until golden-brown. • Baguettes should be served straight from the oven.

Our Tip: *If the risen dough is left in a bowl, covered in clingfilm, overnight, you can shape and bake the bread first thing in the morning.*

Plain White Bread

*Quantities for 1 batch or 1
24cm/10in loaf tin:*
*42g/1¹/₂oz fresh yeast or
21g/3/4oz dry yeast*
1 tbsp sugar
*500ml-750ml/1-1¹/4 pints
lukewarm water*
*1.3kg/2lb 15oz strong plain
flour*
3-4 tsps salt
For the glaze:
2 tbsps milk
2 tbsps stout or malt beer
Butter for tin and baking sheet

Preparation time:
40 minutes
Rising time:
3 hours
Baking time:
50 minutes for the tin, 35–40
minutes for the batch
Nutritional value:
Analysis per slice, if divided
into 40 slices, approx:
• 460kJ/110kcal
• 4g protein
• 0g fat
• 24g carbohydrate

Crumble the fresh yeast and
blend the fresh or dry
yeast with the sugar and
100ml/4 fl oz lukewarm water.
Cover and leave to froth in a
warm place for 15 minutes. •
Sift the flour into a large bowl.
Add the dissolved yeast, salt
and remaining water. Knead
the dough well until it leaves
the bowl clean and is smooth
and elastic. Cover and leave to
rise in a warm place for 2
hours or until doubled in bulk.
• Butter the baking sheet and
loaf tin. • Knead the dough
again and divide in two. Half
fill the tin with dough and
smooth the surface using a wet
metal spatula or palette knife.
Shape the remaining dough
into a long batch, about
6cm/2in in diameter, and place
on the baking sheet. Cover
and leave both loaves to prove
for a further 45 minutes. The
dough in the tin should almost
have reached the top of the tin
by this time. • Place an
ovenproof dish of cold water

in the base of the oven. •
Using a sharp knife, make a
long, ½cm/¼in deep cut
lengthways in the dough in the
loaf tin and brush the top with
milk. Make 4 or 5 cuts across
the top of the batch and brush
with the malt beer or stout. •
Bake the bread on the centre
shelf of a preheated
220°C/425°F/Gas Mark 7
oven for 45 minutes. After 10
minutes remove the water
from the oven and reduce the
temperature to
200°C/400°F/Gas Mark 6. •

Take the batch out of the oven
after 35–40 minutes and leave
to cool on a wire rack. • Bake
the loaf tin for a further 10
minutes and leave to rest in the
oven for 5 minutes after the
oven has been switched off. •
Remove from the tin and
leave to cool on a wire rack. •
This white bread tastes best
when eaten straight from the
oven. White bread that has
been stored in a cool place can
be reheated briefly in the oven
or made into toast.

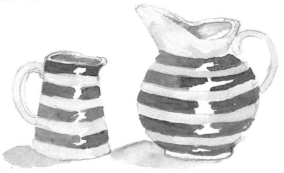

Golden Plaits

Quantities for 2 plaits:
21g/³/₄oz fresh yeast or
10g/¹/₄oz dry yeast
1 tbsp sugar
600ml/1 pint lukewarm milk
1kg/2¹/₄lbs strong plain white
flour
2 tsps salt
100g/4oz soft butter
2 tbsps condensed milk
Butter for the baking sheet

Preparation time:
40 minutes
Rising time:
1³/₄ hours
Baking time:
40 minutes
Nutritional value:
Analysis per slice, if divided
into 30 slices, approx:
• 630kJ/150kcal
• 4g protein
• 4g fat
• 25g carbohydrate

Blend the yeast and sugar with 125ml/4 fl oz milk. Cover and leave to froth in a warm place for 15 minutes. Add the yeast mixture to the flour, the remaining milk, salt and butter and knead to a workable dough. • Cover and leave to rise in a warm place for 1 hour. • Knead the dough again and divide into 6 portions. Place on a lightly floured surface and shape each portion into a 50cm/20in long strip. Lay 3 strips together and make into a plait. Repeat for the second plait. Butter the baking sheet, place the plaits on it, cover and leave to rise for 30 minutes. • Place an ovenproof dish of cold water on the floor of the oven. • Brush the plaits with the condensed milk and bake on the centre shelf of a preheated 200°C/400°F/Gas Mark 6 oven for 40 minutes. Remove the dish of water from the oven after 10 minutes. • Cool the plaits on a wire rack and serve very fresh.

Courgette and Apple Bread

Quantities for 1 30cm/12in loaf:
300g/10oz courgettes
1 medium-sized apple
300g/10oz wheatmeal flour
3 tsps baking powder
5 eggs
100ml/4 fl oz olive oil
1 tsp salt
150g/5½oz freshly grated Cheddar cheese
50g/2oz pumpkin seeds
Butter for the tin

Preparation time:
20 minutes
Baking time:
1 hour 10 min
Nutritional value:
Analysis per slice, if divided into 30 slices, approx:
• 540kJ/130kcal
• 6g protein
• 9g fat
• 8g carbohydrate

Butter the loaf tin. • Coarsely grate the courgette and apple. • Combine the flour, baking powder, eggs, oil, salt, cheese and grated courgette and apple to form a wet dough. Add the pumpkin seeds. • Put the dough in the loaf tin and bake in a preheated 200°C/400°F/Gas Mark 6 oven for 50 minutes. • Reduce the heat to 180°C/350°F/Gas Mark 4 and continue to bake for a further 20 minutes. Leave the bread to cool in the tin, then loosen the edges all the way around using a knife and turn the bread out onto a wire rack.

Our Tip: This apple and courgette bread is very tempting served with raw ham, tomato salad, tzatziki (or cucumber raitha) and wine.

Portuguese Corn Bread

Quantities for 1 30cm/12in tin:
42g/1½oz fresh yeast or
21g/¾oz dry yeast
Pinch of sugar
200ml/7 fl oz lukewarm water
250g/8oz cornmeal
1 tsp salt
200ml/7 fl oz boiling water
1 tbsp olive oil
250g/8oz wheatmeal flour
Butter for the tin

Preparation time:
30 minutes
Rising time:
1¼ hours
Baking time:
40 minutes
Nutritional value:
Analysis per slice, if divided into 25 slices, approx:
• 315kJ/75kcal
• 2g protein
• 1g fat
• 15g carbohydrate

Crumble the fresh yeast, sprinkle the fresh or dry yeast with the sugar and mix with the water. Cover and leave to froth until the cornmeal mixture (see below) has cooled. • Mix 200g/7oz of the cornmeal with the salt and boiling water and leave to cool for 10 minutes. • Add the yeast mixture, the remaining cornmeal, the oil and the wheatmeal flour to the cornmeal mixture and mix well. Knead the dough until soft and elastic, cover and leave to rise for 30 minutes, then knead well and, if necessary, add a little more wheatmeal flour. • Put the dough in the greased baking tin, cover and leave to rise for a further 30 minutes. • Brush the bread with water and bake in a preheated 200°C/400°F/Gas Mark 6 oven for 40 minutes until golden brown.

Turkish Flatbreads

Quantities for 2 flatbreads:
500g/1lb 2oz strong plain flour
1 packet dry yeast
1 tsp salt
1 tsp sugar
100ml/4 fl oz olive oil
250ml/9 fl oz lukewarm water
2 tbsps sesame seeds
Oil for the baking sheet

Preparation time:
30 minutes
Rising time:
1 hour
Baking time:
15-20 minutes
Nutritional value:
Analysis per flatbread, approx:
• 5880kJ/1400kcal
• 29g protein
• 57g fat
• 180g carbohydrate

Combine the flour, dry yeast, salt, sugar and oil. • Slowly add the water. Knead the dough until it is smooth and shiny and leaves the bowl clean. Cover and leave to rise in a warm place for 45 minutes. • Knead the dough well on a lightly floured work surface, shape into 2 balls and roll each out to an oval 1cm/½in thick. • Place the flatbreads on the greased baking sheet, cover and leave to rise for 15 minutes. • Brush the flatbreads with water, prick all over with a fork, sprinkle with the sesame seeds and bake in the centre of a preheated 250°C/480°F/Gas Mark 10 oven for 15-20 minutes until honey-coloured.

Indian Flatbreads

*Quantities for 10 small
flatbreads:*
500g/1lb 2oz floury potatoes
2 medium onions
1 tbsp butter or vegetable ghee
1 bunch of parsley
600g/1lb 5oz wheatmeal flour
½ tsp ground cumin
Pinch of cayenne pepper
1 tsp salt
3 tbsps sunflower oil
250ml/9 fl oz water
*100g/4oz clarified butter or
vegetable ghee*

Preparation time:
1 hour
Baking time:
1¼ hours
Nutritional value:
Analysis per flatbread, approx:
• 1680kJ/400kcal
• 10g protein
• 13g fat
• 64g carbohydrate

Boil the potatoes for 30–35 minutes until cooked; peel and mash while still hot. • Chop and fry the onion in the butter until translucent. • Chop the parsley and combine with the mashed potato, flour, spices, salt and oil. Slowly add the water and then add the cooled onion. • Divide the dough into 12 equal portions and roll out into rounds 15cm/6in in diameter on a lightly floured work surface. • Fry the flatbreads in the clarified butter or ghee in a frying pan over a medium heat for 5 minutes on each side. • Keep the flatbreads warm by covering with aluminium foil and placing in a preheated 75°C/170°F oven until they are all cooked. Serve hot with meat or fish.

Sweet Yeast Bread

Quantities for 1 loaf:
42g/1¹/₂oz fresh yeast or
21g/³/₄oz dry yeast
1 tbsp sugar
200ml/7 fl oz lukewarm milk
100g/4oz currants
4 tbsps rum
650g/1lb 7oz strong, plain
white flour
75g/3oz butter
100g/4oz sugar
1 egg
Pinch of salt
100g/4oz chopped hazelnuts
3 tbsps milk
Butter for the tin

Preparation time:
40 minutes
Rising time:
2¹/₄ hours
Baking time:
25–30 minutes
Nutritional value:
Analysis per slice, if divided
into 40 slices, approx:
• 460kJ/110kcal
• 3g protein
• 4g fat
• 17g carbohydrate

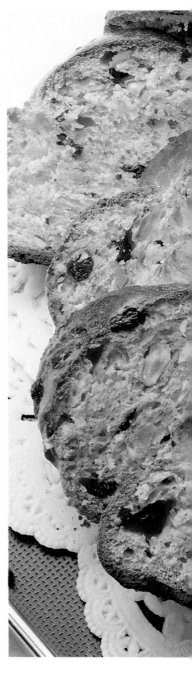

Dissolve the yeast and sugar in 100ml/4 fl oz milk, cover and leave in a warm place to froth. • Wash the currants in hot water, pat them dry and soak them in the rum. • Mix the flour with the yeast mixture and the remaining milk. • Melt the butter and add to the dough together with the sugar, egg, salt, hazelnuts, currants and rum. Knead well until the dough leaves the bowl clean. • Cover and leave the dough to rise in a warm place for 1½ hours. • Butter the baking sheet. • Knead the dough again and divide it into 2 portions. Place them on a lightly floured work surface and roll each into a 50cm/20in strip. Twist the strips of dough around each other in a spiral formation and place on the baking sheet. • Cover and leave to rise for another 30 minutes. • Place an ovenproof dish of cold water in the base of the oven. • Brush the dough with the milk and bake in the centre of a preheated 220°C/425°F/Gas Mark 7 oven for 25-30 minutes. • After 10 minutes remove the dish of water from the oven and reduce the temperature to 200°C/400°F/Gas Mark 6.

Garlic Flatbreads

Quantities for 16 flatbreads:
4 garlic cloves
350g/11oz wholewheat flour
150g/5 ¹/₂oz gram flour
2 tsps salt
¹/₂ tsp white pepper
1 tsp ground cumin
1/2 tsp ground cardamom
200ml/7 fl oz lukewarm water

Preparation time:
20 minutes
Rising time:
8 hours
Baking time:
1 hour
Nutritional value:
Analysis per flatbread, approx:
• 420kJ/100kcal
• 4g protein
• 1g fat
• 22g carbohydrate

Crush the garlic cloves. Place in a bowl and mix with the flours, salt and spices. Add the buttermilk and water gradually, knead the dough well, shape into a ball, wrap it in clingfilm and leave to rise at room temperature for 8 hours. • Knead the dough thoroughly again and divide into 16 equal portions. Shape each slice into a ball, place on a lightly floured surface and roll into a 1cm/¹/₂in thick round. Cook the flatbreads in a dry frying pan or a griddle over a medium to low heat until brown on both sides and then keep them warm in a preheated 75°C/170°F oven until all the flatbreads are ready. • These flatbreads are especially suitable for serving with Indian dishes.

Finnish Flatbreads

Quantities for 8 flatbreads:
350g/11oz wholewheat flour
150g/5¹/₂oz wholemeal rye flour
42g/1¹/₂oz fresh yeast or 21g/¹/₂oz dry yeast
¹/₂ tsp sugar
372ml/14 fl oz lukewarm water
1 tsp salt
4 tbsps oil
For the decoration:
Coarse salt, poppy seeds or sesame seeds
Greaseproof paper for the baking sheet

Preparation time:
30 minutes
Rising time:
1¹/₂ hours
Baking time:
20 minutes
Nutritional value:
Analysis per flatbread, approx:
• 420kJ/100kcal
• 4g protein
• 6g fat
• 39g carbohydrate

Mix the flours, make a well in the centre, crumble the fresh yeast into it and sprinkle with the sugar. Mix half the water and a little flour with the yeast. If using dry yeast, blend the yeast with the sugar, half the water and a little flour and pour it into the well. Cover and leave to rise in a warm place for 15 minutes. Then mix in all the flour, salt, remaining water, 2 tsps oil and knead thoroughly. Shape the dough into a ball, cover and leave to rise for 1 hour. • Line the baking sheet with greaseproof paper. • Knead the dough well, shape into 8 balls and roll each ball out to a 1cm/¹/₂in thick round. Place the rounds on the baking sheet, prick with a fork, brush with the remaining oil and sprinkle with the coarse salt, poppy seeds or sesame seeds. Cover and leave to rise again for 30 minutes. • Bake on the centre shelf of a preheated 220°C/425°F/Gas Mark 7 oven for 20 minutes.

Tangy Aniseed Rolls

Quantities for 12 rolls:
500g/1lb 2oz wheatmeal flour
1 packet dry yeast
Pinch of sugar
1 tsp salt
1 tsp ground aniseed
250ml/9 fl oz lukewarm milk
100g/4oz softened butter
1 egg
1 tbsp condensed milk
1 tbsp each of peeled, chopped almonds and pistachios
Butter for the baking sheet

Preparation time:
20 minutes
Rising time:
1 hour
Baking time:
20-25 minutes
Nutritional value:
Analysis per roll, approx:
• 1000kJ/240kcal
• 7g protein
• 10g fat
• 32g carbohydrate

Combine the flour in a bowl with the yeast, sugar, salt and aniseed. • Add the milk, butter and egg and knead together to form a smooth dough. • Dust the dough with flour and cover. Leave to rise in a warm place for 45 minutes. • Butter the baking sheet. • Knead the dough again, shape into a roll and divide into 12 equal-sized pieces. • Shape the pieces into rolls, lay them on the baking sheet and cover. Leave to rise for a further 15 minutes. • Brush the rolls with the condensed milk; decorate six with the chopped almonds and the rest with the chopped pistachios. Bake the aniseed rolls on the centre shelf of a preheated 200°C/400°F/Gas Mark 6 oven for 20 to 25 minutes until golden.

Crispy Bacon Crowns

Quantities for 12 rolls:
500g/1lb 2oz wheatmeal flour
1 packet dry yeast
Pinch of sugar
¹/₂ tsp salt
250ml/9 fl oz lukewarm milk
100g/4oz softened butter
1 egg
1 onion
200g/7oz rindless streaky
bacon rashers
¹/₂ tsp dried thyme
1 tbsp condensed milk
1 tsp caraway seeds
Butter for the baking sheet

Preparation time:
30 minutes
Rising time:
1 hour
Baking time:
20 minutes
Nutritional value:
Analysis per roll, approx: •
1380kJ/330kcal
• 8g protein
• 20g fat
• 32g carbohydrate

Mix the flour with the yeast, sugar and salt. • Add the milk, butter and egg; knead everything together thoroughly. Cover and leave to rise in a warm place for 45 minutes. • Peel the onions and dice finely. • Cut the bacon into narrow strips and dry fry until the fat begins to run. Add the onion cubes and fry for 2 minutes, then add the crushed thyme. Leave to cool. • Butter the baking sheet. • Knead the dough again, divide into 12 equal-sized pieces, spread them out flat and place the bacon mixture on top. Bring the edges of the dough up round the filling and press firmly. • Arrange the rolls on the baking sheet smooth side up, cover and leave to rise for 15 minutes. • Now make a cross in the top of each roll, brush with condensed milk, sprinkle with the caraway seeds and bake in a preheated 200°C/400°F/Gas Mark 6 oven for 20 minutes.

Peanut Pinwheels

Quantities for 15 pinwheels:
300g/10oz strong plain white
flour
100g/4oz wheatmeal flour
20g/³/4oz soya flour
42g/1¹/2oz fresh yeast or
21g/³/4oz dry yeast
2 tsps runny honey
250ml/9 fl oz lukewarm
buttermilk
1 tsp sea salt
100g/4oz softened butter
100g/4oz unsalted roasted
peanuts
1 egg
1 tbsp each of finely chopped
parsley and chives
Pinch of freshly ground black
pepper
Butter for the baking sheet

Preparation time:
45 minutes
Rising time:
1 hour
Baking time:
25 minutes
Nutritional value:
Analysis per pinwheel, approx:
• 710kJ/170kcal
• 7g protein
• 8g fat
• 19g carbohydrate

Combine the wheat flours with the soya flour. Make a well in the centre. • Crumble in the fresh yeast, add the honey and leave for 2 minutes, or until the yeast has dissolved. If using dry yeast, blend the yeast with the honey and then combine with the flour. • Stir the buttermilk into the yeast mixture with a little flour. Cover and leave to rise for 15 minutes at room temperature. • Stir the starter dough into the rest of the flour, add the salt and 50g/2oz of the butter. Knead the dough thoroughly, cover and leave to rise for a further 20 minutes. • Chop the peanuts and melt the remaining butter. • Butter the baking sheet. • Knead the dough thoroughly and roll out to a 30x40cm/12x16in circle. Brush the dough with the melted butter and beaten egg, sprinkle with the peanuts, herbs and pepper, roll up and cut into slices 2cm/³/4in thick. Arrange the pinwheels on the baking sheet, cover and leave to rise for 25 minutes. • Bake the pinwheels for 20 to 25 minutes in a preheated 200°C/400°F/Gas Mark 6 oven until golden brown, then spray with a little cold water and leave to cool on a wire rack.

Kaiser Rolls

Quantities for 20 rolls:
300g/10oz wheatmeal flour
300g/10oz unbleached strong plain white flour
42g/1¹/₂oz fresh yeast or 21g/³/₄oz dry yeast
3 tsps sugar
350ml/14 fl oz lukewarm water
2 tsps salt
4 tbsps poppy seeds
Butter for the baking sheet

Preparation time:
30 minutes
Rising time:
1½ hours
Baking time:
20-25 minutes
Nutritional value:
Analysis per roll, approx:
• 460kJ/110kcal
• 4g protein
• 1g fat
• 21g/3/4oz carbohydrate

Mix the flours, make a well in the centre, crumble in the fresh yeast and stir in 1 tsp of the sugar, half the water and a little flour. If using dry yeast, blend the yeast with the sugar and water and then pour onto the flour. Cover and leave to rise for 20 minutes at room temperature. • Add the remaining water, flour and salt to the starter dough and knead thoroughly for 10 minutes. • Cover and leave to rise in a warm place for 45 minutes. • Butter the baking sheet. • Knead the dough thoroughly again, shape into a roll and cut into 20 equal-sized pieces. On a lightly floured work surface shape the pieces of dough into balls. Lay the rolls on the baking sheet and, using a sharp knife, make a star pattern on the surface. Cover and leave to rise for 25 minutes. • Stir the remaining sugar into 3 tbsps of water and brush this mixture over the rolls. Sprinkle with the poppy seeds. Place a cup of water on the floor of the oven and preheat the oven to 220°C/425°F/Gas Mark 7. Bake on the centre shelf for 20 to 25 minutes or until golden.

French Table Rolls

Quantities for 20 rolls:
500g/1lb 2oz unbleached
strong plain white flour
42g/1½oz fresh yeast or
21g/¾oz dry yeast
1 tsp sugar
250ml/9 fl oz lukewarm water
80g/3oz butter
1 tsp salt
Butter for the baking sheet

Preparation time:
45 minutes
Rising time:
1¾ hours
Baking time:
25–30 minutes
Nutritional value:
Analysis per roll, approx:
• 500kJ/120kcal
• 3g protein
• 4g fat
• 19g carbohydrate

Sift the flour into a bowl and make a well in the centre. Crumble in the fresh yeast, sprinkle on the sugar and stir with a little water and flour. If using dry yeast, blend the yeast with the sugar and water and then pour onto the flour. • Dust the starter dough with flour, cover and leave to rise for about 20 minutes, until the surface of the flour shows fine cracks. • Melt the butter in the remaining water – if necessary, warm the water slightly. • Stir the flour into the starter dough. Add the liquid gradually and the salt, and knead into a smooth dough. • Cover and leave to rise until it has doubled in bulk – this should take about 1 hour. • Butter the baking sheet. • Knead the dough thoroughly again and cut it into 20 equal-sized pieces; shape some into round and some into long rolls. Cut a lozenge shape in the long rolls and a single groove in the round ones; dust with a little white flour, cover and leave to prove for 20 minutes. • Bake the rolls on the centre shelf of a preheated 220°C/425°F/Gas Mark 7 oven for 25 to 30 minutes or until golden.

Brioches

Quantities for 20 individual brioche tins 8cm/3in in diameter:
750g/1lb 11oz unbleached, strong plain white flour
42g/1½oz fresh yeast or 21g/¾oz dry yeast
50g/2oz icing sugar
125ml/4 fl oz lukewarm milk
200g/7oz butter
5 eggs
1 tsp salt
For the glaze:
2 egg yolks
Butter for the tins

Preparation time:
1 hour
Rising time:
1¾ hours
Baking time:
15-20 minutes
Nutritional value:
Analysis per brioche, approx:
• 1210kJ/290kcal
• 9g protein
• 15g fat
• 30g carbohydrate

Sift the flour into a bowl, make a well in the centre and crumble in the fresh yeast. Stir half the icing sugar and a little milk and flour into the yeast, cover and leave to rise for 15 minutes at room temperature. If using dry yeast, blend the yeast with the sugar and milk and then add to the flour. • Melt the butter and leave to cool. • Stir the eggs into the remaining icing sugar and milk, add the salt and butter, pour the mixture onto the edge of the flour and knead all the ingredients thoroughly with the starter dough. • Cover and leave the dough to rise for 1 hour; it should double in volume. • Grease the tins with butter. • Knead the dough again, shape into a roll and cut into 20 pieces. • Mould each piece into one large and one small ball. Put the larger balls in the tins, make a dip on top of each brioche and press the smaller ball into it. • Beat the egg yolks with 1 tbsp water, brush on the brioches, cover and leave to rise for 30 minutes. • Brush the brioches again with the remaining egg yolk and bake on the centre shelf of a preheated 220°C/425°F/Gas Mark 7 oven for 15 to 20 minutes until golden brown.

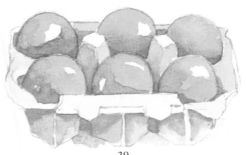

Croissants

Quantities for 15 croissants:
500g/1lb 2oz unbleached,
strong plain white flour
¹/₂ tsp salt
30g/1oz fresh yeast or
15g/¹/₂oz dry yeast
1 tbsp sugar
Just under 250ml/9 fl oz
lukewarm milk
300g/10oz butter
1 egg
For the glaze:
1 egg yolk
1 tbsp single cream
Butter for the baking sheet

Preparation time:
1¹/₂ hours
Rising time:
4 hours
Baking time:
20-25 minutes
Nutritional value:
Analysis per croissant, approx:
• 1380kJ/330kcal
• 7g protein
• 23g fat
• 26g carbohydrate

Sift the flour into a bowl with the salt, make a well in the centre, crumble in the fresh yeast and stir together with the sugar, milk and a little flour. If using dry yeast blend the yeast with the sugar and milk and then add to the flour. Dust the dough with flour, cover and leave in a warm place to rise, until the surface of the flour shows fine cracks – this should take about 20 minutes. • Melt a quarter of the butter and leave to cool. • On a lightly floured work surface, dust the remaining hard butter with flour, roll out to a 15x15cm/6x6in square and place on baking paper in the refrigerator. • Pour the melted butter and egg onto the edge of the flour and mix with the remaining flour and starter dough. Knead the dough for about 20 minutes and knock it back until it is light and elastic. • Cover and leave to rise at room temperature for 45

minutes. • Knead the dough again and, on a floured work surface, roll out to a 20x35cm/8x14in rectangle. Place the chilled butter square on top, folding the dough over it, and refrigerate for 15 minutes. • Now roll out the dough to a 30x40cm/12x16in rectangle, fold the dough into 3, and return to the refrigerator for another 30 minutes. • Repeat this process three more times, rolling out the rectangle and giving it a quarter turn each time, and leaving it to rest in the refrigerator between rollings. • Finally, roll the dough out to 25x80cm/10x32in strips, make a mark with a sharp knife at 10cm/4in intervals and cut triangles with sides 25cm/10in long. On the 10cm/4in short side make a cut 3cm/1in deep in the centre so that the croissant can be shaped more easily. Roll up the triangles towards the central point and shape into crescents. • Butter the baking sheet , lay the croissants on it a reasonable distance apart, cover and leave to prove until they have almost doubled in bulk. This will take about 45 minutes. • Beat the egg yolk with the cream, brush the croissants with the mixture and bake them on the centre shelf of a preheated 220°C/425°F/Gas Mark 7 oven for 20 to 25 minutes or until golden-brown. • Enjoy the croissants at their best, still warm from the oven and spread with chilled butter and marmalade.

Our Tip: *Croissants are extremely versatile. They taste equally delicious with a sweet nutty filling and a savoury stuffing of minced meat, mushrooms and herbs.*

Potato Rolls

Quantities for 15 rolls:
400g/14oz wholewheat flour
42g/1¹/₂oz fresh yeast or
21g/³/₄oz dry yeast
1 tsp sugar
125ml/4 fl oz each of
lukewarm milk and lukewarm
water
2 medium onions
1¹/₂ tbsps butter
100g/4oz smoked ham
125g/5oz cooked potatoes
8 fresh sage leaves
2 tbsps oil
1 tsp salt
Pinch of black pepper
Greaseproof paper for the
baking sheet

Preparation time:
50 minutes
Rising time:
1³/₄ hours
Baking time:
25–30 minutes
Nutritional value:
Analysis per roll, approx:
• 545 kJ/130kcal
• 4g protein
• 5g fat
• 20g carbohydrate

Sift the flour into a bowl, make a well in the centre, crumble in the fresh yeast and sprinkle with the sugar. • Mix the milk with the water and stir a little of it into the yeast with a little flour. If using dry yeast, blend the yeast with the milk and water before adding to the flour. Cover and leave to rise at room temperature for 15 minutes. • Peel and finely chop the onions, and fry until transparent in ¹/₂ tbsp butter. • Cut the smoked ham into small cubes. Mash the potatoes. Chop the sage leaves. • Knead the starter dough with the rest of the flour and the remaining liquid. Add the onions, ham, potatoes, sage, oil, salt and pepper, cover and leave to rise until it has doubled in bulk – this will take about 1 hour. • Line the baking sheet with greaseproof paper. • Knead the dough again, cut into 15 equal-sized pieces and shape into round rolls. • Cover and leave to rise for 30 minutes. • Cut a cross in the top of each roll. Melt the rest of the butter and brush it over the rolls; bake on the centre shelf of a preheated 200°C/400°F/Gas Mark 6 oven for 25 to 30 minutes.

Beer Sticks

Quantities for 32 sticks:
200g/7oz rye flour
200g/7oz wholewheat flour
2 tsps caraway seeds
1 tsp sea salt
2 tbsps sourdough starter mix
½ packet dry yeast
1 tbsp raw cane sugar
200g/7oz lukewarm sour
cream or thick-set plain yogurt
5 tbsps wine vinegar
4 tbsps sunflower oil
Butter for the baking sheet

Preparation time:
40 minutes
Rising time:
1 hour
Baking time:
30 minutes
Nutritional value:
Analysis per stick, approx:
• 230kJ/55kcal
• 2g protein
• 2g fat
• 8g carbohydrate

Mix the flours in a bowl with the caraway seeds, salt, sourdough starter mix, dry yeast and raw cane sugar. • Make a well in the centre, add the sour cream, vinegar and oil and knead to a smooth dough. Cover and leave to rise at room temperature for 30 minutes. • Divide the dough into 32 equal-sized pieces – it is probably best to weigh them. Shape them into balls and, on a floured work surface, roll out to 20cm/8in long sticks. • Cover and leave to rise for 30 minutes. • Butter a baking sheet. • Arrange the beer sticks on the baking sheet and bake on the centre shelf of a preheated 200°C/400°F/Gas Mark 6 oven for 30 minutes until crispy and slightly brittle. • Spray with a little cold water and leave to cool on a wire rack. • These bread sticks will stay fresh for at least a week in an airtight metal container.

Grissini

Quantities for 60 grissini:
500g/1lb 2oz wheatmeal flour
1 tsp salt
50g/2oz fresh yeast or
25g/1oz dry yeast
Just under 200ml/6 fl oz
lukewarm water
1 tsp sugar
6 tbsps olive oil
For the glaze:
Milk
Butter or olive oil for the
baking sheet

Preparation time:
40 minutes
Rising time:
1 hour
Baking time:
15 minutes
Nutritional value:
Analysis per stick, approx:
• 145 kJ/35kcal
• 1g protein
• 1g fat
• 6g carbohydrate

Mix the flour and salt in a bowl. Make a well in the centre, crumble the fresh yeast into it and mix in the water, sugar and a little flour. If using dry yeast, blend the yeast with the sugar and water and pour onto the flour. Cover and leave to rise at room temperature for 20 minutes. • Knead the starter dough with the remaining flour and olive oil to form a smooth dough which leaves the bowl clean. Cover and leave to rise for 30 minutes. • On a lightly floured work surface roll out the dough to a thickness of 2cm/1in and cut into 10cm/4in long fingers. Roll into sticks about 20 to 25cm/8 to 10in long. • Grease or oil the baking sheet. • Lay the grissini on the baking sheet, cover and leave to rise for 10 minutes; then brush with milk. • Bake on the top shelf of a preheated 220°C/425°F/Gas Mark 7 oven for 15 minutes until golden.

Luxury Cheese Assortment

Quantities for 80 biscuits:
250g/8oz wheatmeal flour
1 tsp baking powder
60g/2oz each of Cheddar,
Caerphilly and Camembert
cheese
200g/7oz chilled butter
1 egg
Pinch each of white pepper,
ground nutmeg and sweet
paprika
**For the glaze and
decoration:**
1 egg yolk
1 tbsp cream
1 tbsp each of chopped peanuts,
pistachios, caraway seeds,
poppy seeds and sesame seeds
Greaseproof paper for the
baking sheet

Preparation time:
1½ hours
Standing time:
1 hour
Baking time:
10 minutes
Nutritional value:
Analysis per biscuit, approx:
• 185kJ/45kcal
• 1g protein
• 4g fat
• 2g carbohydrate

Sift the flour and baking powder on to a work surface. • Finely grate the Cheddar and Caerphilly and pass the Camembert through a sieve. Sprinkle the cheese over the flour. Cut the butter into knobs and add to the flour. Break the egg into the centre and sprinkle with the spices. Chop the ingredients, then knead to a smooth shortcrust dough. • Cover and refrigerate for 1 hour. • Line the baking sheet with greaseproof paper. • On a lightly floured work surface roll out the dough in 2 portions to a thickness of 5mm/¼in and either cut out 3cm/1in-sized biscuits or, using a pastry wheel, cut small lozenge shapes. • Beat the egg yolk with the cream. • Lay the first batch of biscuits on the baking sheet, brush with the egg yolk and cream and sprinkle the peanuts, pistachios and poppy, caraway and sesame seeds onto alternate biscuits. • Bake on the top shelf of a preheated 220°C/425°F/Gas Mark 7 oven for 10 minutes until golden.

Cashew Biscuits

Quantities for 70 biscuits:
150g/5¹/₂oz salted cashew nuts
150g/5¹/₂oz wheatmeal flour
100g/4oz chilled butter
1 tsp curry powder
Pinch of salt
1 tbsp crème fraîche
2 egg yolks
2-3 tbsps grated Parmesan
cheese
For rolling out: clingfilm
Greaseproof paper for the
baking sheet

Preparation time:
1¹/₂ hours
Standing time:
1 hour
Baking time:
15 minutes
Nutritional value:
Analysis per biscuit, approx:
• 230kJ/55kcal
• 2g protein
• 5g fat
• 2g carbohydrate

Shell the nuts and mix with the flour. Cut the butter into knobs and add to the flour with the curry and salt. Spoon the crème fraîche and 1 egg yolk into the middle. Chop up the ingredients and knead to a smooth, shortcrust pastry. Cover and refrigerate for 1 hour. • Line the baking sheet with greaseproof paper. • Divide the dough into two portions, lay it on clingfilm and roll it out to a thickness of 3mm/¹/₈in thick. • Cut out 4cm/2in biscuits with a pastry cutter, or use a pastry wheel to cut lozenge shapes. • Beat the remaining egg yolk with 2 tbsps water. • Lay the biscuits on the baking sheet. Brush them with the egg yolk, sprinkle with the Parmesan and bake on the centre shelf of a preheated 200°C/400°F/Gas Mark 6 oven for 15 minutes or until golden.

Spicy Potato Biscuits

Quantities for 40 biscuits:
1kg/2¼lbs floury potatoes
2 garlic cloves
1 bunch of chives
1 tsp salt
Pinch each of ground nutmeg
and black pepper
1 tsp dried marjoram
1 egg
100g/4oz wheatmeal flour
100g/4oz freshly grated
medium mature Cheddar or
Gouda
120g/4½oz chopped sunflower
seeds
For the baking sheet and to
drizzle: 6 tbsps oil

Cooking time:
30-40 minutes
Preparation time:
40 minutes
Baking time:
25-30 minutes
Nutritional value:
Analysis per biscuit, approx:
• 290kJ/70kcal
• 3g protein
• 4g fat
• 6g carbohydrate

Simmer the potatoes in boiling water for 30 to 40 minutes, peel and, while still hot, press through a sieve. • Finely chop the garlic and chives. • Roughly knead the cooled, mashed potatoes with the garlic, nutmeg, pepper, marjoram, chives, egg, flour and cheese to form a light, workable dough. If necessary, add a little more flour. • Brush the baking sheet generously with oil. • With floured hands, divide the dough into about 40 portions and shape into round, flat biscuits. • Roll both sides of each biscuit in the sunflower seeds and press them in gently. • Lay the potato biscuits on the baking sheet, drizzle a little oil over each one and bake on the centre shelf of a preheated 220°C/425°F/Gas Mark 7 oven for 25 to 30 minutes. • Enjoy the biscuits fresh from the oven.

Saffron Turnovers

Quantities for 40 turnovers:
220g/7¹/₂oz wheatmeal flour
220g/7¹/₂oz butter
220g/7¹/₂oz low fat curd cheese
2 pinches of salt
1 sachet ground saffron
1 leek
2 tbsps butter
¹/₂ tsp black pepper
100g/4oz Gorgonzola
2 egg yolks
Greaseproof paper for the baking sheet

Preparation time:
1 hour
Standing time:
45 minutes
Baking time:
15-20 minutes
Nutritional value:
Analysis per turnover, approx:
• 375kJ/90kcal
• 3g protein
• 7g fat
• 4g carbohydrate

Knead the flour with the butter, curd cheese, pinch of salt and saffron. Cover and refrigerate for 45 minutes. • Cut the leek into thin rings and fry in the butter for 5 minutes. Season, leave to cool and combine with the Gorgonzola and 1 egg yolk. • Line the baking sheet with greaseproof paper. • Roll out the dough to a thickness of 5mm/¹/₄in; cut out 40 circles of 7cm/3in diameter and spoon on the filling. Fold up the edges, pressing firmly, and prick each surface once with a fork. • Beat the remaining egg yolk with 1 tbsp water. Brush the crescents with this, place them on the baking sheet and bake on the centre shelf of a preheated 200°C/400°F/Gas Mark 6 oven for 15 to 20 minutes until golden; if possible, serve straight from the oven.

Mini Empanadas

Quantities for 40 empanadas:
250g/8oz wheatmeal flour
250g/8oz each of butter and
low fat curd cheese
Pinch of salt
1 onion
2 preserved chillies
100g/4oz mushrooms
1½ tbsps raisins
1 hard-boiled egg
2 tbsps oil
250g/8oz minced beef
1½ tbsps tomato purée
½ tsp each of salt, black pepper
and dried thyme
Pinch of cayenne
2 eggs
2 tbsps milk
Greaseproof paper for the
baking sheet

Preparation time:
1½ hours
Standing time:
45 minutes
Baking time:
25–30 minutes
Nutritional value:
Analysis per empanada, approx:
• 460kJ/110kcal
• 4g protein
• 8g fat
• 5g carbohydrate

Knead the flour with the butter, curd cheese and salt. Cover and leave in a cool place for 45 minutes. • Finely chop the onions and chillies. Wipe the mushrooms and chop finely. Wash the raisins in hot water. Dice the egg. • Fry the onions in the oil until translucent, add the mince and fry. Add the prepared vegetables, raisins, egg, tomato purée and spices, and cook for 10 minutes. • Line the baking sheet with greaseproof paper. • Separate the eggs. • Roll out the dough extremely thinly, cut out 40 7cm/3in squares. Spoon on the filling, brush the edges with the egg white, fold the squares up into triangles and press the edges firmly. • Beat the egg yolks with the milk and brush on the empanadas; bake in a preheated 200°C/400°F/Gas Mark 6 oven for 25 to 30 minutes.

Olive Pinwheels

Quantities for 24 pinwheels:
21g/³/₄oz fresh yeast or
10g/¹/₄oz dry yeast
Pinch of sugar
125ml/4 fl oz lukewarm water
300g/10oz wheatmeal flour
1 tsp salt
3 eggs
6 tbsps olive oil
100g/4oz almonds
150g/5¹/₂ oz black olives
1 bunch of fresh basil
1 garlic clove
200g/7oz low fat curd cheese
Greaseproof paper for the
baking sheet

Preparation time:
1 hour
Rising time:
1³/₄ hours
Baking time:
25–30 minutes
Nutritional value:
Analysis per pinwheel, approx:
• 585kJ/140kcal
• 6g protein
• 8g fat
• 10g carbohydrate

Dissolve the crumbled fresh yeast or dry yeast in the water with the sugar, cover and leave to froth at room temperature for 15 minutes. • Knead the flour, salt, 1 egg and oil into the yeast mixture, until it is no longer sticky. Dust the dough with flour, cover and leave to rise for 1 hour, until it has doubled in bulk. • Cover the almonds with boiling water and remove their skins. • Stone the olives and chop finely with the almonds. • Chop the basil and garlic finely. • Combine the curd cheese with the almond and olive mixture, 1 egg and the herbs. • Line the baking sheet with greaseproof paper. • Roll out the dough to a 40x40cm/16x16in square; spoon on the curd cheese mixture, leaving a strip of 2cm/1in at one side clear. • Roll the dough up firmly and, using a sharp, floured knife, cut into 24 pieces. Lay the pinwheels on the baking sheet and press them down gently. • Beat the remaining egg and brush onto the pinwheels; cover and leave to rise for 30 minutes. • Bake in a preheated 200°C/400°F/Gas Mark 6 oven for 25 to 30 minutes.

Yeasty Whirls

Quantities for 25 whirls:
21g/³/₄oz fresh yeast or
10g/¹/₄oz dry yeast
125ml/4 fl oz lukewarm milk
Pinch of sugar
250g/8oz wheatmeal flour
Pinch of salt
1 egg yolk
1 tbsp butter
150g/5¹/₂oz smoked sausage
4 sticks celery
1 tbsp oil
1 tbsp chopped walnuts
Pinch of black pepper
Butter for the baking sheet

Preparation time:
1¼ hours
Rising time:
1 hour
Baking time:
20 minutes
Nutritional value:
Analysis per whirl, approx:
• 375kJ/90kcal
• 3g protein
• 6g fat
• 8g carbohydrate

Dissolve the crumbled fresh yeast or dry yeast in the milk and sugar. Cover and leave to froth at room temperature until it has dissolved. • Combine the flour in a bowl with the salt, add the egg yolk, remaining milk and the butter and knead together with the yeast mixture, until the dough leaves the bowl clean. • Cover and leave to rise at room temperature for 1 hour. • Skin and dice the sausage. Finely chop the celery. • Heat the oil and fry the sausage; add the celery and fry briefly. Dry on absorbent paper, then add the walnuts and season with pepper. • Butter the baking sheet. • Roll out the dough to form a 25x35cm/10x14in rectangle and brush on the filling, leaving a 1cm/¹/₂in wide strip all the way round. Roll the dough up from the short end and cut into 25 pieces. • Lay the coils on the baking sheet and bake on the centre shelf of a preheated 200°C/400°F/Gas Mark 6 oven for 20 minutes or until golden brown.

Poppy Seed Pretzels

Quantities for 30 pretzels:
250g/8oz wheatmeal flour
125g/5oz chilled butter
1 egg yolk
1 tbsp crème fraîche
½ tsp each of salt, sweet
paprika and freshly ground
black pepper
3 tbsps black poppy seeds
2 egg yolks
Butter for the baking sheet

Preparation time:
1 hour
Standing time:
40 minutes
Baking time:
15–20 minutes
Nutritional value:
Analysis per pretzel, approx:
• 420kJ/100kcal
• 3g protein
• 7g fat
• 6g carbohydrate

Put the flour in a bowl, cut the butter into knobs and add; then mix in the egg yolk, crème fraîche, salt, paprika and pepper, and knead to form an elastic dough. • Shape into a roll of around 3cm/1in in diameter, cover and refrigerate for 40 minutes. • Butter the baking sheet. • Cut the dough roll into 30 pieces; on a lightly floured work surface shape into 17cm/7in long cylinders and shape these into mini-pretzels. • Pour the poppy seeds onto a plate. Beat the egg yolks with a little water. Brush the egg yolks on the pretzels and turn them gently in the poppy seeds. Arrange them on the baking sheet and bake in a preheated 180°C/350°F/Gas Mark 4 oven for 15 to 20 minutes.

Cheese Parcels

Quantities for 25 parcels:
250g/8oz wheatmeal flour
1 egg
1-2 tbsps lukewarm water
3 tbsps olive oil
Pinch of salt
1 tsp balsamic vinegar
50g/2oz stoned black olives
250g/8oz feta cheese
¹/₂ tsp each of salt and freshly
ground black pepper
1 tsp dried oregano
2 tbsps chopped pistachio nuts
1 egg yolk
100g/4oz melted butter
1 bunch of chives
Butter for the baking sheet

Preparation time:
1 hour
Standing time:
30 minutes
Baking time:
30 minutes
Nutritional value:
Analysis per parcel, approx:
• 545kJ/130kcal
• 4g protein
• 9g fat
• 8g carbohydrate

Put the flour in a bowl. Beat the egg with the water, oil, salt and vinegar, combine with the flour and knead until it is no longer sticky. Cover and refrigerate for 30 minutes. • Chop the olives finely, crumble on the feta cheese and add the salt, pepper, crushed oregano, pistachios and egg yolk. • Butter the baking sheet. • On a floured work surface roll the dough out thinly, to an 80x120cm/32x47in rectangle. If necessary, you can stretch it further, using the backs of your hands. • Brush the melted butter on the rolled out dough. Cut out 25 circles of 8cm/3in diameter and spoon on the filling. Bring the edges up over the filling, pressing together to form little parcels. • Lay the parcels on the baking sheet and bake on the centre shelf of a preheated 180°C/350°F/Gas Mark 4 oven for 30 minutes, basting frequently with the remaining butter. • Wind 1 chive round each cooled parcel as decoration.

Ham Crescents

Quantities for 16 crescents:
500g/1lb 2oz strong plain flour
21g/³/₄oz fresh yeast or 10g/¹/₂oz dry yeast
1 tsp sugar
250ml/9 fl oz lukewarm water
1 tsp salt
2 onions
250g/8oz lean, raw ham
2 tbsps butter
2 tbsps chopped fresh parsley
Pinch of white pepper
1 egg
1 egg yolk
3 tbsps milk
Greaseproof paper for the baking sheet

Preparation time:
1 hour
Rising time:
1 hour
Baking time:
15 minutes
Nutritional value:
Analysis per crescent approx:
• 710kJ/170kcal
• 6g protein
• 5g fat
• 24g carbohydrate

Make a well in the flour, crumble in the yeast and stir in the sugar, a little flour and a little lukewarm water. If using dry yeast, blend with the sugar and water and pour onto the flour. Cover and leave to froth at room temperature for 15 minutes. • Add salt and remaining water to the flour and knead to form a smooth dough. Cover and leave to rise for 30 minutes. • Finely chop onions and ham. • Heat the butter and fry the onions until translucent; add ham and parsley and fry briefly. Remove mixture from the heat, season with the pepper and combine with the beaten egg. • Line the baking sheet with greaseproof paper. • Roll the dough to form 2 circles 36cm/14in in diameter. Cut each circle into 8 triangles; spoon on the filling and shape into crescents by rolling up the triangles. Arrange crescents on the baking sheet and leave to stand for 15 minutes. • Beat the yolk with the milk, brush on the crescents and bake in a preheated 220°C/425°F/Gas Mark 7 oven for about 15 minutes.

Ham and Cheese Diamonds

Quantities for 60 diamonds:
150g/5¹/₂oz wheatmeal flour
150g/5¹/₂oz wholemeal flour
21g/²/₃oz fresh yeast or
10g/¹/₄oz dry yeast
1 tsp sugar
125ml/4 fl oz lukewarm water
2 tbsps butter
¹/₂ tsp salt
1 onion
1 tsp butter
150g/5¹/₂oz each of cooked
and raw ham, fat removed
3 eggs
125ml/4 fl oz single cream
100g/4oz double cream
100g/4oz grated Cheddar
cheese
Butter for the baking sheet

Preparation time:
45 minutes
Rising time:
1¹/₂ hours
Baking time:
40 minutes
Nutritional value:
Analysis per diamond, approx:
• 290kJ/70kcal
• 3g protein
• 5g fat
• 4g carbohydrate

Mix the flours in a bowl, make a well in the centre, crumble in the yeast and stir in the sugar and half the water. If using dry yeast, blend the yeast with the sugar and water and pour onto the flour. Cover and leave to froth at room temperature for 15 minutes. Cover and leave to rise for 15 minutes. • Melt the butter in the remaining water and knead with the salt, starter dough and remaining flour. Cover and leave to rise for 45 minutes. • Chop the onions and fry in the butter until translucent. • Cut the ham into strips. • Beat the eggs with the single and double cream; combine with the ham and onion. • Butter half the baking sheet. • Roll out the dough to the size of half the sheet, place it on the sheet and leave to rise for 30 minutes. • Spoon the ham mixture over the dough; sprinkle on the cheese. • Bake on the centre shelf of a preheated 210°C/410°F/Gas Mark 6 oven for 40 minutes; cut into 60 diamonds.

Bacon Bakes

Quantities for 50 rolls:
400g/14oz fat bacon
Pinch of dried sage
500g/12oz wheatmeal flour
15g/¹⁄₂oz butter
1 tsp salt
Just under 300ml/11 fl oz
cold water
1 egg yolk
Butter and flour for the baking
sheet

Preparation time:
45 minutes
Standing time:
2 hours
Baking time:
12 minutes
Nutritional value:
Analysis per roll, approx:
• 95kJ/95kcal
• 2g protein
• 6g fat
• 7g carbohydrate

Remove the rind from the bacon. Cut the bacon into cubes, mince with the mugwort and cook on a low heat. Strain through a sieve and allow the fat to harden. • Work the flour and butter, salt and water to a stiff dough. Roll it out to a thickness of about 1.5cm/²⁄₃in, in a 32x42cm/12x16in rectangle. • Spoon the bacon fat onto half of the rolled out dough and fold the other half on top. Leave to stand in a cool place for 30 minutes. • Roll the dough out again to a thickness of 1.5cm/²⁄₃in, fold together again and leave to stand in a cool place for a further 30 minutes. • Repeat the whole process again twice at half-hourly intervals. • Butter the baking sheet and dust it with flour. • Roll the dough out again to a thickness of 1.5cm/²⁄₃in and cut out rounds 5cm/2in in diameter. Place them on the baking sheet, brush with the beaten egg yolk and bake in a preheated 200°C/400°F/Gas Mark 6 oven for 12 minutes.

Herb and Cheese Diamonds

Quantities for 1 baking sheet:
200g/7oz rye flour
200g/7oz wheatmeal flour
1 tbsp yeast
2 tbsps sourdough starter mix
About 250ml/9 fl oz
lukewarm water
1 tsp honey
1 tsp salt
2 bunches fresh dill
300g/10oz freshly grated
Parmesan cheese
3 eggs
300g/10oz crème fraîche
Pinch of white pepper
Lard for the baking sheet

Preparation time:
30 minutes
Rising time:
1³/₄ hours
Baking time:
25 minutes
Nutritional value:
Analysis per slice, if divided
into 30 slices, approx:
• 630kJ/150kcal
• 7g protein
• 9g fat
• 12g carbohydrate

Mix the flours with the yeast, sourdough extract, water, honey and salt and knead into a stiff, workable dough. Cover and leave to rise in a warm place, until it has doubled in volume – this will take about 1 hour. • Grease the baking sheet with lard. • Roll the dough out on the baking sheet and prick all over with a cocktail stick. • Pull the leaves off the dill stalks and chop finely. • Combine the Parmesan cheese with the eggs, crème fraîche, pepper and dill and spread over the dough. Cover and leave to rise for 40 minutes. • Bake on the centre shelf of a preheated 200°C/400°F/Gas Mark 6 oven for about 25 minutes.

Savoury Choux Puffs

Quantities for 60 puffs:
250ml/9 fl oz water
150g/5oz butter
Pinch of salt
Pinch of celery salt
175g/6oz wheatmeal flour
3 eggs
400g/14oz calves liver
3 tbsps dry sherry
150g/5¹/₂oz soft butter
¹/₂ tsp each of salt and freshly ground white pepper
3 tbsps chopped chives
Greaseproof paper for the baking sheet

Preparation time:
1 hour
Baking time:
20 minutes
Assembly:
20 minutes
Nutritional value:
Analysis per puff, approx:
• 250kJ/60kcal
• 2g protein
• 4g fat
• 2g carbohydrate

Bring the water to the boil with 100g/4oz of the butter, the salt and celery salt. Add the flour and beat until the dough forms a ball. Transfer to a bowl, leave to cool and beat the eggs into it one by one. • Line the baking sheet with greaseproof paper. • Put the dough in a piping bag with a small star nozzle and pipe 60 balls (about the size of a cherry) on the baking sheet. • Bake on the centre shelf of a preheated 220°C/425°F/Gas Mark 7 oven for 20 minutes or until golden; leave to cool. • Cut the liver into thin strips and brown in the rest of the butter. Cut into cubes and blend in a liquidizer. Combine with the sherry, butter, salt, pepper and chives, and chill until set. • Cut the puffs in half horizontally. Spread the liver paste on the bottom half and pop the lid on top.

Mini-Brioches

*Quantities for 20 4cm/2in
tins:*
250g/8oz wheatmeal flour
15g/¹/₂oz fresh yeast or
8g/¹/₄ oz dry yeast
1 tsp sugar
6 tbsps warm milk
100g/4oz sliced salami
3 tbsps chopped chives
100g/4oz butter
2 eggs
Pinch of salt
Grated rind of 1 lemon
1 egg yolk
2 tsps cream
Butter for the tins

Preparation time:
1 hour
Rising time:
1 hour
Baking time:
15-20 minutes
Nutritional value:
Analysis per brioche, approx:
• 585kJ/140kcal
• 5g protein
• 10g fat
• 9g carbohydrate

Pour the flour into a bowl
and make a well in the
centre. Crumble in the fresh
yeast, mix with the sugar, milk
and a little of the flour. If using
dry yeast, blend it with the
sugar and milk and pour onto
the flour. Cover and leave to
rise for 20 minutes. • Remove
the skin from the salami, chop
into very small cubes and
combine with the chives. Melt
the butter and knead with the
eggs, salt, lemon rind, salami,
remaining flour and starter
dough, until it becomes
smooth and elastic. Cover and
leave to rise for 40 minutes. •
Grease the tins with butter. •
Shape the dough into a roll,
divide into 20 pieces and shape
each into 2 balls, one the size
of a walnut and the other
cherry-sized. • Place the larger
balls in the tins, make an
indentation in the centre and
set the smaller balls on top. •
Beat the egg yolk with the
cream. Brush onto the brioches
and bake in a preheated
220°C/425°F/Gas Mark 7
oven for 15 to 20 minutes.

Index